The Story of a Special Day
Volume 76

March 16

75th day of the year
(76th in leap years)
290 days remaining
until the end of the year.

by Michael Dobson

Timespinner
Press

Table of Contents

Cover: Robert Goddard and the first liquid-fuel rocket, launched March 16, 1926, for the Event of the Day.

Back Cover: The month of March, from the French Gothic illuminated manuscript *Les Très Riches Heures du duc de Berry.*

March 16 Quotations

"The secret of a happy marriage remains a secret."

— *Henny Yougnman, born March 16, 1906*

"A commonplace of political rhetoric has it that the quality of a civilization may be measured by how it cares for its elderly. Just as surely, the future of a society may be forecast by how it cares for its young."

— *Daniel Patrick Moynihan, born March 16, 1927*

"The man who is possessed of wealth, who lolls on his sofa or rolls in his carriage, cannot judge the wants or feelings of the day-laborer. The government we mean to erect is intended to last for ages."

— *James Madison, born March 16, 1751*

"You have been tried by twelve good men and true...and they have said you are guilty. Time will pass and seasons will come and go. Spring with its wavin' green grass and heaps of sweet-smellin' flowers on every hill and in every dale. Then sultry Summer, with her shimmerin' heat-waves on the baked horizon. And Fall, with her yeller harvest moon and the hills growin' brown and golden under a sinkin' sun. And finally Winter, with its bitin', whinin' wind, and all the land will be mantled with snow. But you won't be here to see any of 'em; not by a damn sight, because it's the order of this court that you be took to the nearest tree and hanged by the neck til you're dead, dead, dead, you...son of a billy goat."

— Judge Roy Bean, died March 16, 1903

"In a free state there should be freedom of speech and thought."

— Emperor Tiberius, died March 16, 37

Event of the Day
First Liquid-Fuel Rocket Launched

American professor and inventor Robert H. Goddard, one of the founding fathers of modern rocket science, built and launched the first liquid-fueled rocket on March 16, 1926. He would go on to launch 33 more rockets between 1926 and 1941, reaching a height of almost two miles and speeds in excess of 500 mph.

Rockets themselves, of course, go back a lot farther than 1926. The Chinese, inventors of gunpowder, used them as early as the 1232. The Korean *hwach'a* (화차), or fire cart, first used in the late 14th century, could launch up to 200 small rockets in a single blast.

Europeans learned of rockets and gunpowder in the 12th century. Our word "rocket" is from the Italian *rochetta* (little fuse), an early firecracker.

The Indians used rockets against the British East India Company in 1792, and the British in turn used them against the Americans in the the War of 1812 — the "rocket's red glare" of "The Star-Spangled Banner."

Early science fiction writers Jules Verne and H.G. Wells helped inspire the idea of rockets for use in space travel. In 1903, Russian high school math teacher Konstantin Tsiolkovsky published the first scientific work on the topic.

It was Robert Goddard, however, inspired by Wells, who turned theory into practice. His book *A Method of Reaching Extreme Altitudes*, was not well received, however, receiving a scathing editorial in the New York *Times*. (They published a correction in 1969, right after Apollo 11 took off for the Moon.)

Goddard's breakthrough rocket design spurred research in Germany and Russia, and in less than 20 years, German V-2 rockets, designed by Werner von Braun's team, attacked London and other targets in World War II.

Goddard's work continued. In 1917, he proposed a rocket launcher for infantry that eventually turned into the bazooka. Relocating to Roswell, New Mexico, Goddard continued his research. Unfortunately, the American military took rockets less seriously than did the Germans, and Goddard received few resources. His work was notable enough, however, that the Soviets had an NKVD agent spy on his program, gaining important information in the process.

The esteem that Goddard enjoyed outside the United States was reflected in a remark Werner von Braun made after the war: "Don't you know about your own rocket pioneer? Dr. Goddard was ahead of us all."

Goddard died of throat cancer in 1945, having received over 200 patents for his work. NASA's Goddard Space Flight Center is named for him, as is Goddard Crater on the Moon. A small statue marks the site of his first flight.

Robert Goddard

March 16 Holidays and Celebrations

Bacchanalia (Roman Empire)

Bacchanalia, a festival for the Roman god of wine, Bacchus, was originally a secret revel of women held on March 16 and 17. Men began to join and the wild festival spread until it was being held five times each month! The Roman Senate tried to prohibit the festival beginning in 186 BCE with limited success. Today, the word bacchanalia is used to describe various form of drunken or lustful revelry.

Day of the Book Smugglers (Lithuania)

When Russian Imperial authorities banned Lithuanian language books starting in 1866, book smugglers began to bring in printed material from other countries. There were heavy penalties for book smugglers — some were even shot. Today, the book smugglers are honored — there's even a statue to the "Unknown Book Smuggler." March 16 is the birthday of leading smuggler Jurgis Bielinis. There is a statue honoring the "Unknown Book Smuggler."

Latvian Legion Day (Latvia)

The Latvian Legion was a Waffen-SS unit created in 1943 that fought against the Soviet Union on the side of the Nazis in World War II. The date commemorates the Battle for Hill 93,4 on March 16-18, 1944, in which the Legion defended against a Soviet assault. The day is controversial because of its Nazi connections, but Lithuania claims the Legion only fought against the Soviet Union and was not involved in any other Nazi activities.

St. Urho's Day (Finnish community in the U.S. and Canada)

Finnish-Americans in northern Minnesota established St. Urho's Day in the 1950s to celebrate the mythical Finnish hero who "chased the grasshoppers out of Finland" and saved the grape crop. On his day, people wear royal purple and nile green for grapes and grasshoppers.

Christian Feast Days

Saints commemorated on March 16 include Abbán and Heribert of Cologne.

What Happened on March 16?

The abbreviation "O.S." on some dates refers to the fact that the Russian Empire did not switch from the Julian to the Gregorian calendar at the same time as the rest of Europe, and therefore some figures have two dates for their birth or death.

People whose original names are not in the Western alphabet have their native names in the appropriate script shown in parenthesis.

597 BCE - Nebuchadnezzar Captures Jerusalem

On the second of Adar (March 16), 597 BCE, Nebuchadnezzar II, king of the Chaldean Empire (Babylon), and his forces conquered the kingdom of Judah and captured the city of Jerusalem, beginning the period known as the Babylonian Captivity in Biblical history.

37 CE - Caligula Becomes Emperor

One of the most notorious of the early Roman emperors, Caligula ("little boot") became emperor of Rome at the age of 25 on the death of his great-uncle Tiberius. Although he is described as being a moderate ruler in his first two years on the throne, in later years he acquired a reputation as an insane tyrant, cruel, extravagant, and sexually perverse. He became the first Roman emperor to be assassinated (Julius Caesar was dictator, not emperor). While his assassins hoped to restore the Roman Republic, the Praetorian Guard instead declared Claudius, uncle of Caligula, as the new emperor. The novel and TV miniseries *I, Claudius* tells the story in great detail.

Bust of Caligula

1190 CE - Massacre of the Jews at York

When English monarch Richard the Lionhearted declared his intention to join the Crusades, anti-Jewish sentiment in England flared up, leading to a pogrom against Jews in the city of York. On March 16, 1190, the besieged Jews committed suicide to avoid being killed by the surrouding mob, and set the castle on fire to prevent their bodies from being mutilated. About 150 Jews died in the massacre.

1621 CE - Samoset Greets the Pilgrims

The pilgrims at Plymouth Colony were extremely surprised when a Native American walked straight into their camp and addressed them in English, saying, "Welcome, Englishman! My name is Samoset." This was the first encounter between a Native American and the Pilgrims. Samoset, a member of the Wompanoag tribe, had learned English from fisherman that came to Monhegan Island, Maine. After spending a night with the Pilgrims, Samoset left and returned two days later with Squanto, who would help the Pilgrims recover from their first winter.

Samoset greets the Pilgrims in English

1660 CE - End of the Long Parliament

The Long Parliament was established in 1640 to pass financial bills needed by Charles I, but hostility between the King and Parliament triggered the English Civil War. The Long Parliament finally dissolved itself on March 16, 1660, to be replaced by a new Parliament that would restore the monarchy under Charles II. The Long Parliament is known for many republican reforms, and some credit it with inspiring the American Revolution.

1802 CE - Official Founding of the Army Corps of Engineers

Although military engineers had been part of the Continental Army from the beginnings of the American Revolution, Thomas Jefferson established the Corps of Engineers on March 16, 1802, for the primary purpose of establishing a military academy at West Point. For many years, West Point was the only engineering school in the United States.

1861 CE - Sam Houston Removed From Office

Texas leader Sam Houston, the only man in American history to have been governor of two different states (Tennessee and Texas), opposed Texas's secession from the United States to join the Confederacy, and refused to swear an oath to the new government. He was evicted from office on May 16, 1861.

1912 CE - Lawrence Oates's Sacrifice

The British Antarctic Expedition, also known as the Terra Nova Expedition, was an attempt to be first to reach the South Pole, but were beaten by Roald Amundsen. On the return journey, expedition member Lawrence "Titus" Oates became ill. Rather than burden his teammates, on March 16, 1912, he stepped out of the tent to die, saying "I am just going outside and I may be some time." His sacrifice was in vain; the rest of the team died before the month was out. Search parties later recovered journals, photos, and bodies.

Terra Nova Expedition at the South Pole (standing, from left to right) Edward Wilson, Robert Falcon Scott (leader), Lawrence Oates (sitting, left to right) Henry Bowers, and Lt."Teddy" Evans

1945 CE - Bombing of Würzburg

Toward the end of World War II in Europe, 500 British Royal Air Force bombers attacked the city of Würzburg, Bavaria in an evening attack lasting 17 minutes that killed 5,000 and destroyed 90% of the medieval town center.

1966 CE - Gemini VIII Lifts Off

On March 16, 1966, at 4:41pm Eastern time, Gemini 8, the sixth manned flight in the Gemini program, carrying Neil Armstrong and David Scott, lifted off from Cape Kennedy. It achieved the first docking of two spacecraft in orbit, but a failure of one of the thrusters aboard the spacecraft resulted in the need for an emergency landing, the only time until Apollo 13 that a planned mission was aborted before its end.

1968 CE - My Lai Massacre

On March 16, 1968, American soldiers led by platoon leader 2nd Lieutenant William Calley, killed at least 347 unarmed South Vietnamese in the hamlets of My Lai and My Khe. Out of 26 soldiers accused in the massacre, only Calley was found guilty by court martial in a controversial trial, but served only 3-1/2 years of a life sentence.

1984 CE - Kidnapping of William Buckley

On March 16, 1984, Hezbollah operatives kidnapped Beirut CIA chief William Buckley. He underwent 15 months of torture before being executed by Islamic Jihad on October 4, 1985.

1985 CE - Kidnapping of Terry Anderson

One year exactly after the kidnapping of Buckley, Hezbollah kidnapped journalist Terry Anderson and held him for six years and nine months. Anderson was released on December 4, 1991. He successfully sued the Iranian government for his kidnapping, receiving a multi-million dollar settlement from frozen Iranian assets.

1988 CE - Iran-Contra Indictments

On March 16, 1988, National Security Advisor John Poindexter and National Security Council member Oliver North were indicted on charges related to the Iran-Contra scandal. Both were found guilty, but their convictions were reversed because of Fifth Amendment issues related to their testimony before Congress.

1988 CE - Halabja Poison Gas Attack

During the final days of the Iran-Iraq War, On March 16, 1988, Saddam Hussein ordered the use of chemical weapons against the Kurdish town of Halabja, killing at least 3,200 and injured at least 7,000 more. The largest chemical weapons attack against a civilian population in history, the Halabja attack has been declared a genocidal attack against the Kurdish people by the Iraqi Special Tribunal for Crimes Against Humanity and by courts in the Netherlands.

1995 CE - Mississippi Abolishes Slavery

The 13th Amendment to the U.S. Constitution, outlawing slavery, was rejected by Mississippi in an 1865 vote. On March 16, 1995, Mississippi became the last state to ratify the amendment.

Who Was Born on March 16?

Acting and Film

Brooke Burns (March 16, 1978 —)

Actress and former model Burns appeared on *Baywatch* and *Baywatch Hawaii.*

Paul Schneider (March 16, 1976 —)

Schneider played Mark Brendanawicz on two seasons of *Parks and Recreation* and won a Best Supporting Actor Award from the National Society of Film Critics for his role in *Bright Star.*

Sienna Guillory (March 16, 1975 —)

Guillory played the title role in the 2003 TV miniseries *Helen of Troy,* the elf princess in *Eragon*, and Jill Valentine in several films in the *Resident Evil* series.

Tim Kang (March 16, 1973 —)

Kang played Kimball Cho in the TV series *The Mentalist.*

Alan Tudyk (March 16, 1971 —)

Tudyk played Wash in *Firefly,* Steve the Pirate in *DodgeBall: A True Underdog Story,* and co-starred in the ABC sitcom *Suburgatory.*

Judah Friedlander (March 16, 1969 —)

Friedlander (below) is best known as the hat-wearing Frank in the sitcom *30 Rock.*

Lauren Graham (March 16, 1967 —)

Graham played Lorelai on *Gilmore Girls* and Sarah on *Parenthood*.

Gore Verbinski (March 16, 1964 —)

Verbinski is best known for directing the *Pirates of the Caribbean* film series and the Academy Award-winning animated feature *Rango*.

Kevin Tod Smith (March 16, 1963 — February 15, 2002)

Australian actor Kevin Smith played Ares, the god of war, in the TV series *Hercules: The Legendary Journeys, Xena: Warrior Princess,* and *Young Hercules*.

Bruno Barreto (March 16, 1955 —)

Brazilian director Barreto is known for such films as 1976's *Dona Flor and Her Two Husbands* and 1997's *Four Days in September.*

Graham Cole (March 16, 1952 —)

Cole appeared in numerous *Doctor Who* serials, including Melkur in "The Keeper of Traken."

Joseph Pilato (March 16, 1949 —)

Pilato played the psychotic Captain Rhodes in 1985's *Day of the Dead.*

Victor Garber (March 16, 1949 —)

Garber played Jesus in *Godspell*, Jack Bristow in *Alias*, and Thomas Andrews in James Cameron's *Titanic*.

Erik Estrada (March 16, 1949 —)

Estrada is best known as the co-star of the TV series *CHiPs*.

Chuck Woolery (March 16, 1941 —)

Game show host Chuck Woolery is known for such programs as *Love Connection*. He was the original host of *Wheel of Fortune*.

Bernardo Bertolucci (March 16, 1940 —)

Bertolucci is best known as the director of *Last Tango in Paris* and *The Last Emperor*.

Olga San Juan (March 16, 1927 — January 3, 2009)

Known as the "Puerto Rican Pepperpot," San Juan appeared in films with Bing Crosby, Fred Astaire, and others.

Jerry Lewis (March 16, 1926 —)

Legendary comic and director Jerry Lewis is known for his films, his partnership with Dean Martin, and his charity fund-raising telethons for muscular dystrophy.

Dean Martin (top) and Jerry Lewis (bottom)

Leo McKern (March 16, 1920 — July 23, 2002)

Leo McKern's best known role was as the title character in the BBC series *Rumpole of the Bailey.* He is also known for his role as Number Two in the 1960s cult classic *The Prisoner.*

Mercedes McCambridge (March 16, 1916 — March 2, 2004)

Academy Award and Golden Globe winning actress McCambridge appeared in *All the King's Men, Johnny Guitar*, and *Giant.* She provided the voice for the possessed child in the movie *The Exorcist.*

Robert Rossen (March 16, 1908 — February 18, 1966)

Rossen is known as the director of *All the King's Men, The Hustler,* and other films. He was blacklisted by the House Un-American Activities Committee, but subsequently named 57 people and was removed from the blacklist.

Henny Youngman (March 16, 1906 — February 24, 1998)

Violin-playing comic Henny Youngman is perhaps best known for his one-line joke, "Take my wife — please."

Conrad Nagel (March 16, 1897 — February 24, 1970)

Nagel was a matinee idol of the silent film era, helped found the Academy of Motion Picture Arts and Sciences, and later hosted the popular 1950's TV game show *Celebrity Time.*

Conrad Nagel and Renée Adorée in 1928's *The Michigan Kid*

Art

Todd McFarlane (March 16, 1961 —)

Comic book artist McFarlane first achieved fame with his work on Marvel's *Spider-Man.* He created the anti-hero *Spawn* and also designs toys.

Antoine-Jean Gros (March 16, 1771 — June 25, 1835)

Painter Antoine-Jean Gros is known for his many paintings of Napoleon, several of which hang in Versailles.

Napoleon on the Battlefield of Eylau by Antoine-Jean Gros

Business

Sandy Weill (March 16, 1933 —)

Banker Sanford Weill was chief executive of Citigroup.

**Shibusawa Eiichi (渋沢 栄) (March 16, 1840
— November 11, 1931)**

Eiichi is known as the "father of Japanese
capitalism" after the Meiji Restoration. He
founded the first modern bank in Japan.

Chess

Michael Basman (March 16, 1946 —)

International chess master Michael Basman is
best known for his contributions to the field of
chess openings.

Modeling

Tiiu Kuik (March 16, 1987 —)

Estonian fashion model Tiiu Kuik has modeled
for over 50 designers, has been on multiple
Vogue covers, and represented CoverGirl
cosmetics.

Nicole Trunfio (March 16, 1986 —)

Australian model Nicole Trunfio served as
mentor for female models in the second season
of *Make Me A Supermodel*.

Music

Wolfgang Van Halen (March 16, 1991 —)

Son of guitarist Eddie Van Halen and actress Valerie Bertinelli, Wolfgang Van Halen plays bass for the rock group Van Halen.

Maher Zain (ماهر زين) (March 16, 1981 —)

Muslim Swedish-Lebanese singer Maher Zain had an international hit in the Muslim world with 2009's *Thank You Allah.*

Tracy Bonham (March 16, 1967 —)

Alternative rocker Bonham is known for her 1996 single "Mother Mother." She received two Grammy nominations in 1997.

Flavor Flav (March 16, 1959 —)

William Drayton, Jr., rose to prominence as the rapper Flavor Flav with Public Enemy, and has appeared on a number of reality series. He is known for wearing large clocks around his neck when he performs.

Nancy Wilson (March 16, 1954 —)

Nancy Wilson is part of the rock band Heart.

Fred Neil (March 16, 1936 — July 7, 2001)

Songwriter Fred Neil is known for "Everybody's Talkin," recorded by Harry Nilsson for the movie *Midnight Cowboy*.

John Addison (March 16, 1920 — December 7, 1998)

Addison scored such films as *A Bridge Too Far, A Taste of Honey, Sleuth*, and *Torn Curtain*. He wrote the theme music for the TV series *Murder, She Wrote*. He won both an Academy Award and a Grammy for his music for the 1963 film *Tom Jones*.

Newsmakers

Traudl Junge (March 16, 1920 — February 10, 2002)

Junge was Adolf Hitler's private secretary from 1942 to Hitler's suicide in 1945.

Tsutomu Yamaguchi (山口 彊) (March 16, 1916 — January 4, 2010)

Yamaguchi is the only person recognized as having survived the atomic bombings of both Hiroshima and Nagasaki.

Josef Mengele (March 16, 1911 — February 7, 1979)

Auschwitz physician Josef Mengele, called the "Angel of Death," supervised incoming transports of prisoners to determine which ones would be put to death immediately, and performed human experiments on other camp inmates, including children. He escaped to South America after the war and evaded capture for the rest of his life.

Matthew Flinders (March 16, 1774 — July 19, 1814)

British Royal Navy captain Matthew Flinders was the first person to circumnavigate Australia and correctly identify it as a continent. He suggested the name "Australia."

Politics and Government

Comrade Feliciano (March 16, 1953 —)

Óscar Ramírez, better known as Comrade Feliciano, was a leader of the Peruvian organization Shining Path, a Maoist group. He was captured in 1999 and sentenced to life in prison.

Daniel Patrick Moynihan (March 16, 1927 — March 26, 2003)

Sociologist and politician Moynihan was senator from New York, and held ambassadorial and other roles in four consecutive presidential administrations, from JFK to Gerald Ford. He was also known for his scholarly and popular books.

Pat Nixon (March 16, 1912 — June 22, 1993)

Pat Nixon, wife of President Richard Nixon, was First Lady of the United States from 1969 to 1974.

Richard and Pat Nixon on the beach at San Clemente, 1971

Mike Mansfield (March 16, 1903 — October 5, 2001)

A U.S. senator from Montana, Mike Mansfield was the longest-serving Senate Majority Leader in history.

James Madison (March 16 [O.S. March 5], 1751— June 28, 1836)

James Madison (left) was the fourth President of the United States and is called the "Father of the Constitution" for his work on that document and on the Bill of Rights.

Science and Technology

Richard Stallman (March 16, 1953 —)

Software freedom activist Stallman launched the GNU free software movement and serves as president of the Free Software Foundation.

Philippe Kahn (March 16, 1952 —)

Kahn founded four technology companies: Fullpower Technologies, Starfish Software, LightSurf Software, and Borland. He set a trans-Pacific sailing record of under 8 days.

Ursula Goodenough (March 16, 1943 —)

Biologist Goodenough is best known for her best-selling *Sacred Depths of Nature* and appears in PBS and History Channel productions.

Amos Tversky (עמוס טברסקי) (March 16, 1937 — June 2, 1996)

Tversky is known for his innovative work with Daniel Kahneman on cognitive science, cognitive bias, and the handling of risk. His partner won the 2002 Nobel Prize in Economics for their joint work, but the prize is not awarded posthumously.

Raymond Damadian (March 16, 1936 —)

Armenian-American physician Damadian invented the the MRI scanner. He received a National Medal of Technology and is a member of the National Inventors Hall of Fame.

Walt Cunningham (March 16, 1932 —)

Cunningham was the lunar module pilot for Apollo 7.

Crew of Apollo 7 (left to right) Donn Eisele, Wally Schirra, Walt Cunningham

Vladimir Komarov (Влади́мир Комаро́в) (March 16, 1927 — April 24, 1967)

Cosmonaut Komarov commanded the first multi-manned Soviet spaceflight and was chosen to command the Soviet attempt to reach the Moon first. He was the first person to die during a spaceflight when Soyuz 1 crashed after re-entry.

Frederick Reines (March 16, 1918 — August 26, 1998)

Reines won the 1995 Nobel Prize in Physics for his co-detection of the neutrino.

Alexander Stepanovich Popov (Алекса́ндр Степа́нович Попо́в) (March 16 [O.S. March 4], 1859— January 13, 1906 [O.S. December 31, 1905])

Popov was the first person to demonstrate the practical application of electromagnetic radio waves and built the first radio receiver.

Georg Ohm (March 16, 1789 — July 6, 1854)

German physicist Georg Ohm did pioneering work on the newly-developed electrochemical cell, and developed Ohm's Law. The unit of electrical resistance, the *ohm*, is named for him.

Caroline Herschel (March 16, 1750 — January 9, 1848)

Caroline Herschel was the sister of astronomer Sir William Herschel and an important astronomer in her own right. Her growth was stunted by typhus, and her family arranged for her to be a house servant. Instead, as an astronomer, she discovered eight comets and the second companion of the Andromeda Galaxy, and organized the 1798 *Catalogue of Stars*, correcting numerous errors in earlier catalogues. She was the first woman presented with a gold medal by the Royal Astronomical Society, and has a crater on the Moon named for her.

Caroline Herschel.

Sports

Blake Griffin (March 16, 1989 —)

Los Angeles Clippers forward Blake Griffin played for the University of Oklahoma, where he was selected as Naismith College Player of the Year and received the Oscar Robinson Trophy. He was named NBA Rookie of the Year in 2011 and by *Sports Illustrated* as one of the 15 greatest NBA rookies of all time.

Kenny Dykstra (March 16, 1986 —)

WWE wrestler Ken Doane won the World Tag Team Championship and appeared on the reality show *Seducing Cindy.* He wrestled as Kenny Dykstra, Ken Phoenix, and Stan Shooter.

Curtis Granderson (March 16, 1981 —)

Center fielder Granderson won the Silver Slugger Award in 2011, and the Marvin Miller Man of the Year Award in 2009. He played for the New York Yankees and the Detroit Tigers.

Todd Heap (March 16, 1980 —)

Tight end Heap was named NFL Alumni Tight End of the Year in 2003 and was an All-Pro selection in 2003. He has played for the Baltimore Ravens and the Arizona Cardinals.

Ozzie Newsome (March 16, 1956 —)

Former Cleveland Browns tight end Ozzie Newsome became general manager of the Baltimore Ravens. He is an inductee into the Pro Football Hall of Fame.

Hollis Stacy (March 16, 1954 —)

LPGA veteran Stacy was elected to the World Golf Hall of Fame in 2011.

Joe DeLamielleure (March 16, 1951 —)

Pro Football Hall of Famer DeLamielleure was best known as part of the Buffalo Bills' "Electric Company" offensive line.

Writing/Books

Kate Worley (March 16, 1958 — June 6, 2004)

Kate Worley co-wrote the alternative comic book *Omaha the Cat Dancer.*

Alice Hoffman (March 16, 1952 — June 6, 2004)

Hoffman is known for her 1996 novel *Practical Magic,* adapted into a movie with the same name.

Margaret Weis (March 16, 1948 —)

Fantasy author Margaret Weis is best known for her work on the *Dragonlance* series with Tracy Hickman.

Sid Fleischman (March 16, 1920 — March 17, 2010)

Fleischman won the Newberry Medal in 1987 for *The Whipping Boy* and wrote biographies, novels, children's books, and books on magic.

Jurgis Bielinis (March 16, 1846 — January 18, 1918)

Bielinis was one of the main organizers of illegal book-smuggling in Lithuania. His birthday is celebrated in that country as the Day of the Book Smugglers.

Sully Prudhomme (March 16, 1839 — September 6, 1901)

French poet Sully Prudhomme won the first Nobel Prize in Literature.

Who Died on March 16?

Acting and Entertainment

Ivan Dixon (April 6, 1931 — March 16, 2008)

Ivan Dixon was best known for playing the communications specialist in the TV series *Hogan's Heroes*.

Anthony George (January 9, 1921 — March 16, 2005)

George starred in the 1960s TV series *Checkmate,* played two roles on *Dark Shadows*, and was Dr. Will Vernon on *One Life to Live*.

Norma McMillan (September 15, 1921 — March 16, 2001)

Canadian voice actor McMillan was Gumby, Casper the Friendly Ghost, and Davey on *Davey and Goliath*.

Charlie Barnett (September 23, 1954 — March 16, 1996)

Barnett played Noogie Lamont on TV's *Miami Vice* and Tyrone in the 1983 film *D.C. Cab*.

Arthur Godfrey (August 31, 1903 — March 16, 1983)

One of the most famous radio and television personalities of the 1940s and 1950s, Arthur Godfrey was known for his folksy style, his ukulele playing, and for the controversial on-air firing of Julius LaRosa.

From left to right: Bing Crosby, Perry Como, Arthur Godfrey

Art

Constantin Brâncuşi (February 19, 1876 — March 16, 1957)

Romanian-born French sculptor Constantin Brâncuşi is famous for such works as "The Kiss," "Bird in Space," and "The Endless Column." A pioneer of modernism, he has been called the "patriarch of modern sculpture."

Aubrey Beardsley (August 21, 1872 — March 16, 1898)

Beardsley is best known for his black ink drawings in the style of Japanese woodcuts. He was an important member of the Aesthetic movement and contributed to the development of art noveau.

Chess

Aron Nimzowitsch (Аро́н Нимцо́вич) (November 7, 1886 — March 16, 1935)

Russian-Danish chess master Nimzowitsch was a leading member of the hypermoderns and an important and influential writer on chess.

Oriental Dancer.

"Oriental Dancer" by Aubrey Beardsley

42

Crime and Punishment

Marvin "Popcorn" Sutton (October 5, 1946 — March 16, 2009)

Moonshiner Marvin "Popcorn" Sutton self-published a guide to moonshine production and self-produced a home video of his activities. His story was put into the documentary The Last One, which won a regional Emmy, and footage from his activities was included in the Moonshiners television series. He committed suicide rather than serve a federal prison sentence for his activities. Country star Hank Williams, Jr., marketed "Popcorn Sutton's Tennessee White Whiskey" named for him.

Judge Roy Bean (c. 1825 — March 16, 1903)

Known as "The Law West of the Pecos," saloon-keeper and justice of the peace Roy Bean (left) was the subject of a 1956 television series and the 1972 movie *The Life and Times of Judge Roy Bean*, starring Paul Newman.

Literature

Selma Lagerlöf (November 20, 1858 — March 16, 1940)

The first female to win the Nobel Prize in Literature, Lagerlöf is best known for her children's book *The Wonderful Adventures of Nils*.

Military

Thomas Ferebee (November 8, 1918 — March 16, 2000)

Ferebee was the bombardier aboard *Enola Gay*, the B-29 that dropped an atomic bomb on Hiroshima, Japan.

Sergeant Stubby (1916/1917 — March 16, 1926)

Stubby was the most decorated war dog of World War I and the only dog to be promoted to sergeant through combat. He once caught a German spy by the seat of his pants.

Sergeant Stubby

Music

Johnny Cymbal (February 3, 1945 — March 16, 1993)

Cymbal is known for his 1963 hit "Mr. Bass Man."

T. Bone Walker (May 28, 1910 — March 16, 1975)

Blues guitarist T. Bone Walker was an innovator of the jump blues and electric blues, and was rated by *Rolling Stone* magazine as one of the 100 greatest guitarists of all time.

T. Bone Walker

Tammi Terrell (April 29, 1945 — March 16, 1970)

Motown artist Terrell is best known for her duets with Marvin Gaye, including "Ain't No Mountain High Enough" and "Ain't Nothing Like the Real Thing."

Politics and News

Richard Wirthlin (March 15, 1931 — March 16, 2011)

Pollster Richard Wirthlin was best known as Ronald Reagan's chief strategist.

Rachel Corrie (April 10, 1979 — March 16, 2003)

American peace activist Rachel Corrie was crushed to death by an Israel Defense Forces armored bulldozer while protesting IDF demolitions of Palestinian homes in the Gaza Strip.

John Hoagland (June 15, 1947 — March 16, 1984)

Photojournalist Hoagland was killed while photographing Salvadoran soldiers. The character "John Cassidy" in the 1986 movie *Salvador* is loosely based on him.

Fred Rose (December 7, 1907 — March 16, 1983)

Canadian Communist politician Fred Rose was the only member of the Canadian Parliament convicted of spying for a foreign country.

Jean Monnet (November 9, 1888 — March 16, 1979)

French economist and diplomat Jean Monnet is considered one of the founding fathers of the European Union.

Kamal Jumblatt (كمال جنبلاط) (December 6, 1917 — March 16, 1977)

Lebanese Druze politician Jumblatt led the Lebanese National Movement. He was assassinated by unidentified gunmen, and was succeeded by his son Walid Jumblatt.

Thomas E. Dewey (March 24, 1902 — March 16, 1971)

Dewey (right, center) was governor of New York State and two-time Republican nominee for president. He is remembered for the 1948 Chicago *Tribune* newspaper headline that erroneously read, "Dewey Defeats Truman."

Marguerite Durand (January 24, 1864 — March 16, 1936)

French actress and journalist Marguerite Durand was a leading suffragette. She was famous for walking her pet lion on Paris streets. Her collection of papers forms the Bibliothèque Marguerite Durand, one of the best sources in the world for research in women's history and feminism.

Anne Neville (June 11, 1456 — March 16, 1485)

Best known to history as a character in three scenes of William Shakespeare's *Richard III*, Lady Anne Neville was Princess of Wales as the wife of Edward of Westminster, and Queen of England as the wife of King Richard III.

Tiberius (November 16, 42 BCE — March 16, 37 CE)

Tiberius Julius Caesar Augustus (below) became the second Emperor of Rome following the death of his adoptive father Augustus Caesar. He was known as "the gloomiest of men." His successor was Caligula.

Science and Space

G. David Low (February 19, 1956 — March 16, 2000)

Astronaut Low flew on three Space Shuttle missions. His father had been manager of the Apollo Spacecraft Program Office.

Derek Barton (September 8, 1918 — March 16, 1998)

Nobel-winning chemist Derek Barton's work on conformational analysis earned him a knighthood. He is the namesake of the Barton reaction, Barton decarboxylation, and Barton-McCombie deoxygenation.

Yves Rocard (May 22, 1903 — March 16, 1992)

Rocard is known as the father of the French A-bomb and H-bomb.

John James Rickard a (September 6, 1876 — March 16, 1935)

Nobel Prize-winning biochemist Macleod was one of the discoverers of insulin.

Nathaniel Bowditch (March 26, 1773 — March 16, 1838)

Mathematician Nathanial Bowditch is considered the father of modern maritime navigation. Every commissioned U.S. Navy ship carries a copy of his book *The New American Practical Navigator*, often referred to simply as "Bowditch."

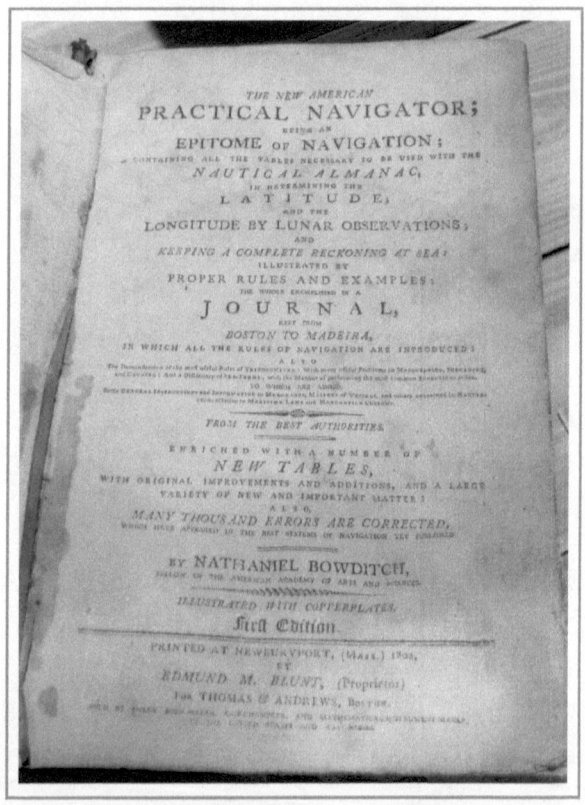

Title page of the first edition of Nathaniel Bowditch's *The New American Practical Navigator*, 1802

Sports

Dick Radatz (April 2, 1937 — March 16, 2005)

Relief pitcher Radatz, known as "The Monster" or "Moose" was named Fireman of the Year twice by *The Sporting News*. He was the first pitcher in baseball history to have consecutive 20-save seasons.

Eddie Shore (November 25, 1902 — March 16, 1985)

Boston Bruin and New York American ice hockey defenceman won the Hart Trophy four times and was elected to the Hockey Hall of Fame in 1947.

March: The Third Month

In ancient Rome, March was the first month of the year. As the first month of spring, in the Mediterranean climate it marked the beginning of the military campaign season. That's why March (Martius) is named in honor of Mars, the Roman god of war.

Although the first month of the year was moved back to January sometime during the transition of Rome from a kingdom to a republic (historians differ), March was the first month of the year in Russia until the end of the 15th Century, and is the first month of the year in many other cultures and religions.

In the northern hemisphere, March 1 marks the beginning of meteorological spring. In the southern hemisphere, March is the equivalent of September, making southern hemisphere March the beginning of autumn.

March is one of the seven months that have 31 days in it. March starts on the same day of the week as November every year, and except for leap years starts on the same day as February.

March starts on the same day of the week as the previous June except for leap years, and in leap years starts on the same day as the previous September and December.

March in Other Cultures

In Finland, March is called *maaliskuu* (earthy month). In Ukraine, it's *березень* (birch tree). Other names for March include *Lentmonat* (Saxon), *Hyld-monath* (Angles), and *sušec* (Slovene).

March Symbols

Birthstones: Aquamarine (below) and bloodstone, both representing courage.

Birth Flowers: Daffodils

Daffodils in Bagatelle Park, Paris, France

March Events

Honorary months: Presidents, Congresses, and nations around the world issue proclamations recognizing particular months to honor certain causes. These events generally fall in March. (All US unless otherwise noted.)

- National Nutrition Month

- American Red Cross Month

- Women's History Month (celebrated in Canada during October)

- Irish-American Heritage Month

- Colorectal Cancer Awareness Month

- Fire Prevention Month (The Philippines)

"March Madness": (United States) The NCAA Men's Division I Basketball Championship, popularly known as "March Madness" or the "Big Dance," is a single-elimination tournament to establish the champion college basketball team.

Multi-day events: Some March events span multiple days.

- **Nineteen Day Fast:** (Bahá'í Faith) March 2 through March 20

- **Girl Scout Week:** (U.S.) The week that includes March 12, the date of the founding of the first chapter of the Girl Scouts of the USA in 1912. The earliest Girl Scout Week can start is March 6, and the latest it can end is March 18. The Sunday of Girl Scout Week is celebrated by some churches as Girl Scout Sunday or Girl Scout Sabbath.

- **Multiple Sclerosis Awareness Week:** (U.S.) Sponsored by the National Multiple Sclerosis Society, MS Awareness Week is normally held on the second full week in March. The earliest it can begin is March 9 and the latest it can end is March 21.

Movable events: Some events change dates from year to year.

- **Passion Sunday:** The fifth Sunday of the Christian season of Lent is known as Passion Sunday in various Protestant denominations and by some traditionalist Catholics. Sometimes, the sixth Sunday of Lent is referred to as Passion Sunday, but it is more commonly known as Palm Sunday. Passion Sunday starts the two week Passiontide, which ends on Holy Saturday, the day before Easter, commemorating the day that Jesus's body was laid in the tomb. The fifth Sunday of Lent can occur as early as March 8 (though the next time it will be that early is in 2285 CE), and as late as April 11.

- **Palm Sunday:** The moveable feast of Palm Sunday commemorates the triumphant entry of Jesus into Jerusalem, an event mentioned in all four gospels. In many Christian churches, palm leaves are distributed to the worshippers. The earliest date for Palm Sunday is March 15, and the latest is April 18.

The month of March, from the illuminated manuscript *Les Très Riches Heures du duc de Berry*

March Zodiac Signs

From the perspective of someone on Earth, the Sun appears to move through the sky throughout the year, along a path astronomers call the ecliptic plane. The ecliptic plane is divided into twelve constellations, known as the zodiac, based on traditionally observed patterns of stars. On your birthday, you can't see your constellation, because it's part of the daytime sky.

The zodiac was first developed by Babylonian astronomers about 2,500 years ago. Because they were unaware that the Earth wobbles like a spinning top (a motion known as *precession*), they didn't make allowance for the fact that the Sun's path through the zodiac changes over time.

That means there are now two sets of dates for your birth sign. The tropical dates are the original Babylonian dates; the siderial dates tell you where the Sun actually appears as it moves along its annual path.

March 16 is one of the few days that has the same astrological sign in both systems: Pisces.

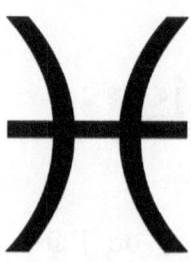

Pisces

Tropical February 20 to March 20

Siderial March 15 to April 14

In the Roman legend of Venus and her son Cupid, they escaped the clutches of Typhon, known as the "father of all monsters," by transforming into fish and tying themselves together with rope. That's why the name Pisces is plural for fish. The constellation appears as a somewhat ragged "V" shape, representing the rope, with the "fish" located at the two rope ends.

In astrology, Pisces is a water sign, compatible with the other water signs Cancer and Scorpio, as well as with the earth signs Taurus, Virgo, and Capricorn. Pisceans are supposed to be imaginative, compassionate, unworldly, secretive, and escapist.

What Day of the Week is March 16?

On what day of the week does March 16 fall?

Surprisingly, this isn't an easy question. Because the calendar year is 365 days long (366 in leap years), it doesn't divide evenly by the seven days of the week.

Also, the Earth goes around the Sun in about 365-1/4 days, so a calendar tends to drift over time. That's why the same date falls on different weekdays in different years.

This is made even more complicated by a change in calendars that took place in 1582. Our modern calendar has its roots in ancient Rome, in a calendar reform conducted by Julius Caesar. Caesar commissioned mathematicians to attack the problem, and came up with the idea of *leap years,* and thus standardized the calendar for centuries to come. This was called the *Julian calendar.*

Over time, however, the small errors in Caesar's calculation compounded. That's why Pope Gregory XIII commissioned the *Gregorian calendar,* used in most of the world today. Some countries converted in 1582, when the calendar was first developed; some converted later; other still haven't changed.

Gregorian and Julian aren't the only types of calendars. The Hebrew year, the Islamic year, and many other calendars are used in different parts of the world and among different people.

You can convert Gregorian dates to other calendars, including the Hebrew calendar, the Islamic calendar, and even the Mayan calendar by visiting the Fourmilab Calendar Converter at http://www.fourmilab.ch/documents/calendar/.

A 50-year brass perpetual calendar.

Copyright, Credit, and Contact

Follow Us

Our blog Dobson's Improbable History features short articles on events and people associated with each day, and updates several times each week. Get the latest on Twitter @SidewiseThinker.

Sources and Art Credits

All art and photographs are either in the public domain or used under a Creative Commons license. Attribution is provided where requested by the copyright owner or when of historical significance, listed below.

- The cover photograph of Robert Goddard and his rocket is by Esther C. Goddard and is used here under the terms of the Creative Commons Attribution-Share Alike 3.0 Unported license.

- The photograph of Robert Goddard at the blackboard is in the public domain as a work of NASA. It is part of the "Great Images in NASA History" collection.

- The photograph of the bust of Caligula was taken by "Clio20" and is used under the Creative Commons Attribution-Share Alike 3.0 Unported license. The bust itself is in the collection of the Louvre Museum in Paris.

- The drawing of Samoset speaking English to the Pilgrims is from a collection in the Sutro Library, San Francisco. It is in the public domain because its copyright has expired.

- As a creation of the U.S. federal government, the Army Corps of Engineers logo is in the public domain.

- The photograph of Sam Houston (approx. 1865) was produced by the studio of Mathew Brady. It is in the public domain because its copyright has expired.

- The photograph of the Terra Nova Expedition is in the public domain because its copyright has expired.

- The photograph of the Gemini 8 capsule after splashdown is in the public domain as a work of NASA.

- The photograph of Judah Friedlander at the 2008 Tribeca Film Festival was taken by David Shankbone, and is used here under the Creative Commons Attribution 3.0 Unported license.

- The photograph of Dean Martin and Jerry Lewis from the *Colgate Comedy Hour* is in the public domain because it was published between 1923 and 1977 without a copyright notice.

- The lobby card for the 1928 film *The Michigan Kid* is in the Beinecke Rare Book & Manuscript Library at Yale University, and is used here under the Creative Commons Attribution-Share Alike 2.0 Generic license.

- The painting *Napoleon on the Battlefield of Eylau* by Antoine-Jean Gros is in the Toledo Museum of Art. The image is part of the Google Art Project and is in the public domain because its copyright has expired.

- The photograph of the Nixons on the beach at San Clemente is in the collection of the Richard Nixon Presidential Library and Museum, and is in the public domain as a work of the U.S. government.

- The portrait of James Madison is by John Vanderlyn, and is in the collection of the White House Historical Association. It is in the public domain because its copyright has expired.

- The lithograph of Caroline Herschel is in the public domain because its copyright has expired.

- The 1950 publicity photo of Bing Crosby, Perry Como, and Arthur Godfrey is in the public domain because it was published between 1923 and 1977 without a copyright notice.

- The drawing "Oriental Dancer" by Aubrey Beardsley is in the public domain because its copyright has expired.

- The photograph of Judge Roy Bean is in the public domain because its copyright has expired.

- The photograph of Sergeant Stubby is in the public domain because its copyright has expired.

- The 1972 photograph of T. Bone Walker at the American Folk Blues Festival in Hamburg, Germany, was taken by Heinrich Klaffs and is used here under the Creative Commons Attribution-Share Alike 2.0 Generic license.

- The 1948 photograph of Thomas E. Dewey is part of the New York *World-Telegram & Sun* collection at the Library of Congress Prints and Photographs Division. Per deed of gift, all rights in this photograph were deeded to the public upon its donation to the Library.

- The painting of Queen Anne Neville is by an unknown artist. It is in the public domain because its copyright has expired.

- The portrait bust of Emperor Tiberius is in the Ny Carlsberg Glyptotek, Copenhagen. This photograph is in the public domain because it was released by the author and copyright holder.

- The photograph of the title page of the first edition of Bowditch's *American Practical Navigato*r was taken by Daderot and released into the public domain by the photographer. The original manuscript is in the HistoryMiami Museum, and is in the public domain because its copyright has expired.

- The illustration of the month of March used on the back cover and in the interior is from the French Gothic illuminated manuscript *Les Très Riches*

Timespinner
Press